Dream Apartments

Dream Apartments

Aurora Cuito

HARPER DESIGN

An Imprint of HarperCollins*Publishers*

DREAMS APARTMENTS
Copyright © 2000 by HARPER DESIGN and LOFT Publications

First published in 2000 by:
HBI, *An Imprint of* HarperCollins*Publishers*

Published in 2004 by:
Harper Design,
An Imprint of HarperCollins*Publishers*
10 East 53rd Street
New York, NY 10022
Tel.: (212) 207-7000
Fax: (212) 207-7654
HarperDesign@harpercollins.com
www.harpercollins.com

Distributed throughout the world by:
HarperCollins International
10 East 53rd Street
New York, NY 10022
Fax: (212) 207-7654

HarperCollins books may be purchased for educational, business, or sales promotional use.
For information, please write: Special Markets Department, HarperCollins Publishers Inc.,
10 East 53rd Street, New York, NY 10022

Publisher: **Paco Asensio**

Editor: **Aurora Cuito**

Text: **Belén García and Alejandro Bahamón**

Art Director: **Mireia Casanovas Soley**

Layout: **Diego González and Ilana Anger**

Copy Editor: **Raquel Vicente Durán**

ISBN: 0-688-18038-8

Library of Congress Control Number: 2004108395

Printed by: Anman Gràfiques del Vallès
DL: B-4821-05
Second Printing, 2005

The purpose of *Dream Apartments* is to offer readers an overview of this kind of dwelling, at the threshold of the 21st century, through a choice selection of projects embracing both architecture and interior design.

The apartments featured in this book—most of which belong to the urban context and reflect a wide variety of needs, clients, authors, and locations—provide a comprehensive sample of city lifestyles. Furthermore, the dwelling is probably one of the architectural forms most sensitive to changes in society, since it responds in an immediate, explicit way to the innermost needs and desires of the individual. And the projects included here are no exception to this rule.

At some stage in their existence, many cities have been on the edge of collapse due to a lack of infrastructures capable of sustaining all the complexities of contemporary life. Traffic congestion, the absence of green zones, the disintegration of the family nucleus, loneliness, noise, and pollution are just some of the factors that make the city an inhospitable place that is alien to its individual inhabitants.

Parallel to this, and in inverse proportion to the progressive increase in the distance between the city and its citizens, the importance of the dwelling has grown as the center around which the life of city dwellers revolves. Besides fulfilling its function as a refuge, it is usually a space conceived for one or more individuals, and consequently designed according to their wishes and requirements.

The sacred place of the urbanite, a sheltering haven, an oasis in the midst of chaos, a multipurpose space that offers the possibility of private life and coexistence with others, the apartment is one of the primary needs of the human individual among the confusion and anonymity of the metropolis. While neutralizing the effects of uniformity, it provides the individual with a small corner in which to recognize him/herself.

The common denominator of all of the apartments featured here is the fact that they are "made to measure"—in other words, conceived according to the client's personal, family, and work circumstances. In some cases, for example, the arrangement of the owners' personal property (paintings, sculptures, objets d'art, or furniture) forms a fundamental part of the project; in others, the apartment becomes a center of operations in that it is both the client's home and his or her workplace.

The versatility that characterizes most of these projects guarantees the apartment dwellers a certain margin of adaptability, essential when it comes to confronting the insecurity of contemporary life. In some cases, flexibility is even a requirement, as is the case of the projects that reutilize old buildings and transform them into dwellings.

Dream Apartments offers readers the possibility to "inhabit" some of today's most spectacular apartments and to identify with the desires and aspirations of their creators. In short, to dream.

Apartment in Casa Magarola

Bárbara Salas
Barcelona, Spain
Photography: Montse Garriga

This apartment was created when a 19th-century former seminary in Barcelona's old quarter was renovated. Casa Magarola —as the building was originally called— had large balconies, very high ceilings, a carriage entrance, and an extensive central courtyard. The transformation of this building into an apartment complex is part of the strategic plan for the renewal of many formerly depressed areas of the city. Making the most of the original building's fine structural features, the renovation converted it into apartments that are small but of ample proportions, with good lighting and a peaceful ambience.

The interior designer took full advantage of the building's unique features, very similar to those of a typical loft, without adopting the minimalist approach often seen in these types of homes. She relied heavily on the choice of materials and colors to create an atmosphere with character. Using the colors of the existing

beams as a reference point, she chose iroko wood furniture with contrasting polished stainless steel frames. The bookshelves and stairs, in the same stainless steel, were conceived as superimposed elements, more like furniture than integral parts of the architecture. Two large wooden sliding doors can be used to integrate the kitchen and pantry with the rest of the space or close them off.

Special attention was paid to the selection of colors and the lighting that, in this case, were crucial for the desired overall effect. Black was used for the sofas and long drapes, and red for the decorative accents, such as the Moroccan rug, vases, and artwork. The lamps were chosen not just for their design, but also because the brightness of each can be controlled independently, in accordance with the client's needs.

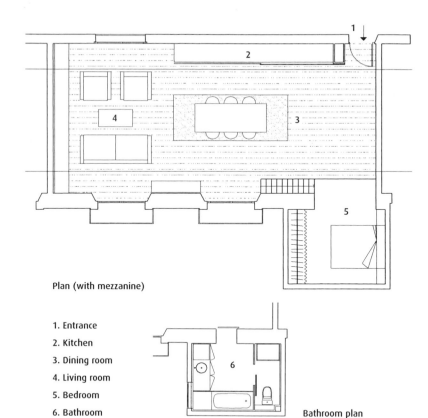

Plan (with mezzanine)

1. Entrance
2. Kitchen
3. Dining room
4. Living room
5. Bedroom
6. Bathroom

Bathroom plan

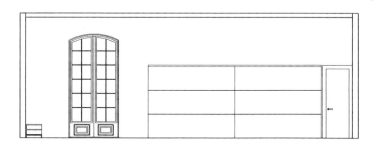

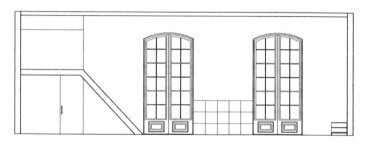

Sections

At one end of the apartment, the high ceilings were used to their best advantage, with the bathroom being placed below the bedroom. The sheet metal used in constructing the loft, a decorative touch in and of itself, was left open to view.

Apartment in Casa Magarola

Formal unity

Guillermo Arias
Bogotá, Colombia
Photography: Eduardo Consuegra, Pablo Rojas

This apartment occupies a large part of what was once a traditional residence in a building in Bogotá dating to the 1930s. Two architects, who collaborate on various projects, decided to remodel the space to create a personal residence for each of them. Architect Guillermo Arias' residence, seen here, was originally made up of several rooms, but it was structurally possible to clear the space in order to form only one room with ample proportions. The starting point for the project was the building's location: close to the city center, but on a tranquil, tree-lined street.

Since the apartment is located on the top floor of the building, the architect envisioned an operation that would modify the roof in various ways in order to enrich the space by responding to the different lines of sight. The architect rebuilt the original exterior balcony that faces the tree-lined street and had been torn down. The slope of one of the roofs was also altered,

generating a longitudinal window in the entire upper part of the apartment that illuminates the back of the space. Finally, the architect moved the ceiling back in one of the rooms to create an interior patio that leads to the bedroom and isolates it from the immediate neighbors. Next to the entrance are a sink and a toilet, on an elevated platform, hidden behind a curved wall that leads to the main space.

Once in this large room, various architectural elements differentiate each zone and give it character. The original chimney was pulled away from the lateral walls and opened on both sides. It now integrates and divides the kitchen and the living room. An axis of rectangular columns is detached from the foyer and demarcates the space for a large bookshelf elevated off the floor. A cabinet containing sound and video equipment indicates the entrance to the bedroom. The space that once housed two bathrooms was merged to make one bathroom, with grand proportions and a closet. The design of the woodwork emphasizes the horizontal lines and helps to blend the different zones. The furnishings and the lamps, designed by the architect, unify the formal language of the residence.

Final details

The design and careful elaboration of each piece in this space creates a continuous and harmonic atmosphere. The furnishings, such as the desk that acts as the study and the dining room table, the bed, and the shelves of the kitchen and the bookshelf, adapt themselves to each circumstance while creating a common language for the entire project.

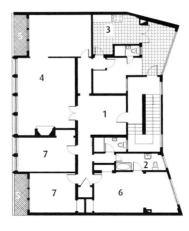

Previous
floor distribution

1. Entry
2. Bathroom
3. Kitchen
4. Dining Room
5. Terrace
6. Bedroom
7. Child's room

Present
floor distribution

1. Entry
2. Bathroom
3. Kitchen
4. Dining Room
5. Terrace
6. Bedroom
7. Library
8. Closet
9. Courtyard

The design of the woodwork, in the windows as well as in the shelves of the library, is adapted to the space. The exit to the terrace features large sections of solid wood that give this element solidity.

Guillermo Arias

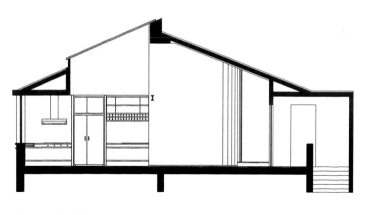

Transversal section

Formal unity

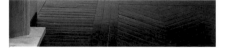

The floors made of wood tablets were preserved from the original residence, but were treated with natural dyes in order to create a darker color.

A continual path

Luis Cuartas
Bogotá, Colombia
Photography: Eduardo Consuegra

This project, together with the previous one, form part of an integral reformation that two architects carried out on an old building in the center of Bogotá. The architects transformed the space into their personal residences. This particular project occupies the part of the building that previously contained the kitchen, the services, and the dining room.

Both projects share certain conditions, including the structure of the building and the tree-lined setting. These circumstances inspired similar operations in terms of alterations to the roof, an opening toward the tree-lined street, and the clearing of the interior space. On the other hand, each architect's distinct needs and architectural concepts brought about very different living spaces. After demolishing the existing walls, the architects envisioned the location of the new pieces that make up the residence. The goal was to create a continual space with diverse relationships between the different areas, and a circular, continual path that covers the entire residence. After crossing the entryway, the circulation offers two alternatives. On the left side, a table extends all the way to the door and invites entry into the kitchen. On the right side, a corridor containing a large bench and a bath integrated with the chimney, leads to the living room, which features unexpectedly high ceilings. From here, a steel stair leads to a walkway where there is a small studio linked to a terrace. The chimney is open on both sides and paves the way to a more intimate zone with shorter ceilings, which opens onto the balcony and overlooks the tree-lined street. After crossing the bedroom and the closet, the path ends, arriving once again at the kitchen.

An elevated platform under the kitchen and bathroom conceals the installations and enriches the relationship between the spaces. The materials define the character of each zone. In the entryway, the smooth, painted cement floor continues until a wood dais in the more intimate area replaces it. The steel and glass structure of the walkway creates an aspect of lightness, while the walls that make up the interior volumes give a sensation of solidity. The mixture of textures and surfaces makes this residence a rich space with a continual path.

 ## Textures

The great formal expressiveness of each corner of this interior is accentuated by the different textures that are achieved through the careful mix of materials. Concrete, green marble, brick, wood, steel, and glass combine harmoniously to give each space its own personality.

The disk storage cabinets and the bookshelves form part of the interior architecture. This careful design emphasizes the play of surfaces and textures.

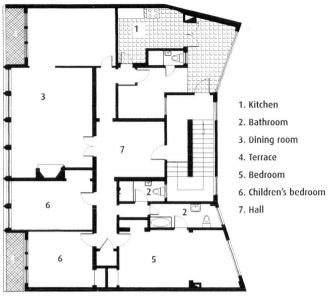

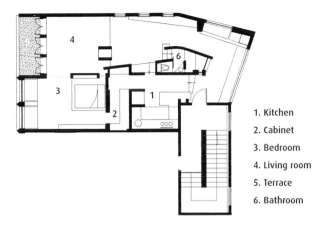

1. Kitchen
2. Bathroom
3. Dining room
4. Terrace
5. Bedroom
6. Children's bedroom
7. Hall

1. Kitchen
2. Cabinet
3. Bedroom
4. Living room
5. Terrace
6. Bathroom

Previous floor distribution

Present floor distribution

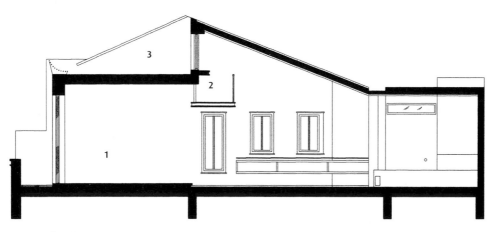

Transversal section

1. Living room
2. Studio
3. Terrace

Attic for a publicist

Arthur de Mattos Casas
São Paulo, Brazil
Photography: Tuca Reinés

The apartment occupies the two top floors of a São Paulo building, and was designed for a famous publicist. Due to the fact that the number of occupants fluctuates, the dwelling was divided into three different zones. In the first place, the area serves the children who sporadically occupy these rooms. This includes the bedrooms and a room for the television and computer. This same floor accommodates the living area, salon, dining room, kitchen, and wash place. The floor above houses the client's private quarters, joined to a terrace with a swimming pool. The project involved no conceptual effort as far as domestic programs are concerned. Efforts here were directed toward placing different works of art and collector's pieces. The main objective was that all of these elements should be placed flexibly, without cluttering space—altering it while also embellishing it. Hence the fact that the pictures are hung from rails by steel cables that may be easily displaced. Furthermore, the objects were put into display cabinets so they would not obstruct the overall visual effect and would be highlighted as they deserve, thanks to specific protection and lighting in each case.

The staircase linking both floors consists of a white-painted metal structure to which wooden steps were attached. Although the materials and finishes coincide with those of the dwelling, this element appears sculptural and confers character on the space.

The wood-and-glass display cases are the solution to the problem of storage and exhibition of valuable objects. Thanks to these elements, it was possible to display the objects in all their splendor while preserving their fragility. The initial objective was to avoid cluttering tables and sideboards, leaving them free for other functions.

Arthur de Mattos Casas's architectural studio not only conceived of the space, but also produced some of the furniture elements for the project, in this case the rug and the dining room table. The apartment also contains design pieces: the dining room chairs are by Charles Eames, the lamp by Pierre Chareau, and the sofa by Jean-Michel Frank.

The client's private quarters have a landscaped terrace with views of the city. Due to the weight that the structure supporting the swimming pool and the plants had to bear, it had to be considerably reinforced.
The studio on this level contains a fireplace, an office, and a bookcase.

Artur de Mattos Casas

Photographer's apartment

Tanner Leddy Maytum, Stacy Architects
San Francisco, United States
Photography: Stan Musilek, Sharon Reisdorph

This photographer's apartment is an expansion of an existing industrial structure located on San Francisco's Potrero Hill. The owner had previously converted this former paint factory into his own photography studio. Later on, he decided he wanted to have the option of living there—in order to enjoy the advantages of its structure and location—but in a space separate from the work area. The original building consisted of a basic rectangular unit with structural walls of concrete block and a roof built on a framework of wooden beams. The new home, superimposed on the original structure, enjoys splendid views of the city and the bay.

The apartment is laid out as part of a series of spaces, one after the other. The studio is located on the ground floor, followed by a mezzanine and the upper floor, where the living space is located, with the roof serving as an outdoor terrace. Thus, the spaces become brighter and more open as one ascends from the closed, dark photography studio.

Tanner Leddy Maytum, Stacy Architects

The narrow exterior balcony and large windows make for fabulous panoramic views of the city and San Francisco Bay.

Axonometric view

1. Entrance/kitchen
2. Bathroom
3. Living room/dining room
4. Bedroom
5. Terrace

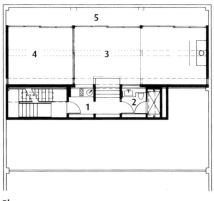

Plan

Photographer's apartment

The kitchen and the bathroom are on a level slightly below the main space, but they are visually connected to the higher level.

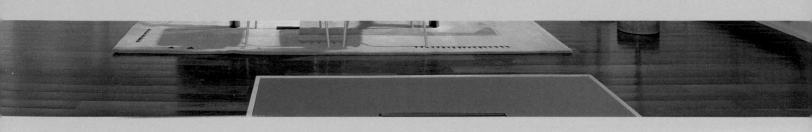

A dwelling in Barcelona

Franc Fernández
Barcelona, Spain
Photography: Joan Mundó

The remodeling of this building transformed what had formerly been a factory-warehouse into a residence. By leaving intact the original height of 14.5 feet, the architect maintained the building's industrial character, at the same time endowing the new apartments with a very marked personality.

Each floor was divided into four spaces of 1,620 square feet. The apartment described here, of 1,190 square feet, is the product of having subdivided one of these spaces. It has the further advantage of occupying a corner of the building, which guarantees natural light throughout. The owner is an actress, which conditioned the kind of space required. Thus, the apartment needed space in which not only to rehearse, but also to give performances. Spaciousness, luminosity, and versatility therefore became the priority objectives of the project. The existing structure was respected: the metal pillars and girders, the floor-ceiling structure of ceramic vaults, and even the large original windows. The floor was divided into two zones: on the one hand, and in a single space, the kitchen, dining room, and living room; and on the other, the bedroom, bathroom, toilet, the studio. The former zone, the more public of the two, has the original high ceilings and enjoys most of the light. In the latter, however, an intermediate ceiling structure was added that divides the space in half vertically. Beneath this new structure, the more private rooms create a feeling of seclusion and intimacy. Above, an open space 5 feet high accommodates the library. This new floor and the original one below are linked by a wooden staircase.

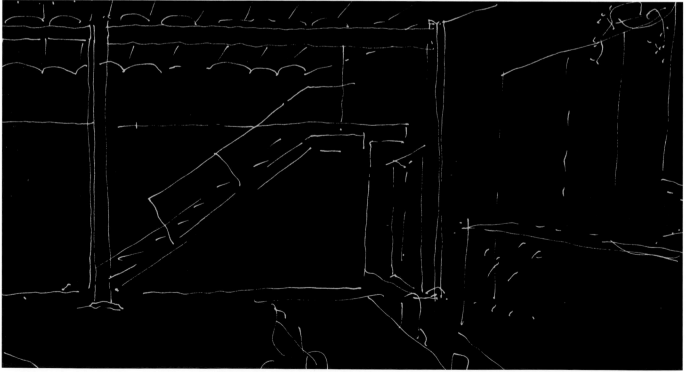

A dwelling in Barcelona

Exploiting an industrial past

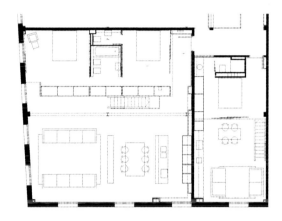

Luminosity, serenity, and intimacy

The walls and ceilings of the apartment have been painted entirely in white, highlighting the original structure. The note of color, however, is to be found on the library floor, on which the beams of light play and from which reflections of the blue industrial paint bounce off in all directions. The floor of the apartment is entirely in solid ipe wood. This wood, which provides a touch of warmth—very necessary in an apartment of these dimensions—coexists in turn with a decor that emphasizes the building's industrial origins, such as the halogen lamps or the wooden staircase, reminiscent of the ladders used on-site.

Intelligence and imagination offset a modest budget

The volume that contains the bedroom, bathroom, toilet, and studio is clad inside in water-varnished beech wood. The space inside the bathroom is visually increased by mirrors. The rooms are connected via sliding doors, some of which are of translucent glass, which means that the square footage of distribution is reduced to a minimum. Franc Fernández has here achieved an apartment in which limited resources were no obstacle to a wealth of solutions. This is further evidence of the fact that even a modest budget can yield an elegant result.

Franc Fernández

Flexible integration

Siggi Pfundt/Form Werkstatt
Munich, Germany
Photography: Karin Heßmann/Artur

Located in the center of Munich, this apartment forms part of what was previously a sewing machine factory in the city's old industrial area. The German architect renovated the space as a private residence. The project had three goals: to give the space flexibility, to preserve its original character, and to employ basic, easily constructed materials and methods for the reformation.

In order to divide the apartment, the architect installed five modular birch plywood panels that hang from a metal rail. These elements accentuate the longitudinal axis of the unit and separate the private and social zones. As a result, the bedroom—differentiated from the rest of the environment by its wood floor—can remain isolated from the living room and work area, or it can become part of the large open space. The social and work zones are grouped along the façade in order to make the most of the space's only source of light. The circulation of the panels along the rail gives the space structure. The panels also control the flow of natural light toward the most intimate part of the residence, located at the back. This visual division preserves the apartment's sensation of amplitude and its dimensions.

For furnishings, the architect used industrial pieces of furniture found in informal stores and souks, like the recycled gas pump used to store the dishes or the office filing cabinets used to store clothing. An old freight elevator found on the site was incorporated into the wall as a shelf. The cement floor alludes to the industrial spirit of the old factory and mixes with the wood and metal to create warmth in this factory-turned-apartment.

The ingenious and flexible use of panels preserves the apartment's continuity and characteristics as much as possible, while resolving the practical considerations, all within a modest budget.

Mobile panels

To maneuver the panels with ease and give the renovation a warm image, the architect opted to use birch plywood. Since the panels are attached only to the upper part, metallic platens are used as reinforcements. They give the elements rigidity and help to support them.

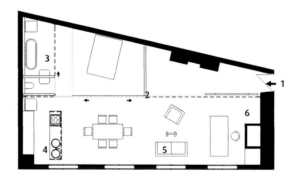

1. Entry
2. Bedroom
3. Bathroom
4. Kitchen
5. Dining room
6. Work area

Plan

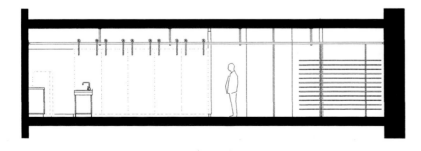

Longitudinal section

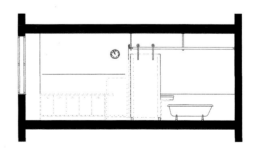

Transversal section

Flexible integration

The central table, in the same tone as the birch plywood panels, blends with the warm-toned furnishings to create a cozy environment that preserves the characteristics of the industrial space.

Loft in London's Soho

Knott Architects
London, United Kingdom
Photography: Jefferson Smith, Laurent Kalfala, Knott Architects

The empty shell of a loft may cause consternation among many clients. Open spaces with no functional differentiation and underestimation of available space mean that some potential purchasers are easily put off. The result of such fear is often the wish to divide the loft into traditional rooms, which spoils its spatial potential.

Knott Architects was faced with the challenge of fitting two bedrooms, two bathrooms, a kitchen, and a living room into 1,296 square feet in a refurbished building in London's Soho. The success of the firm's endeavour, without compromising the integrity of the space, is thanks to a stringent design philosophy, which makes a clear, permanent distinction between inserted elements and the containing shell.

The floors and the service strip that runs along the whole length of the apartment are in maple. On the other hand, the partitions do not disguise the versatility of plywood, showing it exactly as it is. Constructional details have been scrupulously conceived, and include the visible fixing elements, the exposed edges of wooden boards, and the shadows cast by interruptions between materials. All these details together constitute an integral structure.

Loft in London's Soho

Flows of light and air

The bedrooms are understood as pieces of furniture that touch neither the ceiling nor the party walls, except on the glazed edges of the partitions. All interventions are in wood, steel, and glass, thus distinguishing the new construction from the existing walls, plastered and painted white. The partitions are highlighted by a wooden dais that covers the entire floor and conceals the installations beneath.

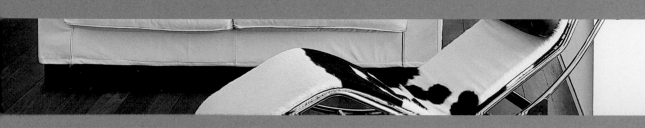

Loft in Plaza Mayor

Manuel Ocaña del Valle
Madrid, Spain
Photography: Alfonso Postigo

This project involved an irregularly formed apartment in an old building located in the center of Madrid. The structure was disorganized and had suffered significant damage and numerous "patch" renovations. The load-bearing walls were wide and presented variable strokes. The passageways were badly defined, and there were angles and projections that made it difficult to move around in a space with such great depth.

The architect restructured the space by creating a regular and orthogonal order. He reorganized the circulations in a space fragmented by sustaining walls that have an important structural function and also organize the space. The new distribution divided the loft into two large zones: a large, open one for the primary living space, and another one, with similar dimensions, that was broken down into smaller areas. A criterion for the renovation of these spaces was to respect the structural elements, since the overall

state of the building was poor. The circulation was reorganized so the resident can appreciate the space as a whole. The materials and textures used for the remodeling reflect the concepts of the apartment's new structure. Woodwork was eliminated in order to free the apartment from the weight of its surroundings. Woodwork and metallic veneers for the furnishings and the doors were used to waterproof the humid zones. This project strengthened the role of the load-bearing walls. Not only structurally functional, they also organize the space. An irregular series of opaque and thick dividing panels gives the loft a new spatial distribution.

Transparencies

The relationships between the different spaces, the bedroom and the study, or the television room and the living room, are achieved with transparent elements, such as glass, or a simple curtain that can divide each zone. The decorative palette, in light tones, also unifies the space and emphasizes the feeling of spaciousness.

1. TV room
2. Kitchen
3. Dining room
4. Bedroom
5. Studio

Plan

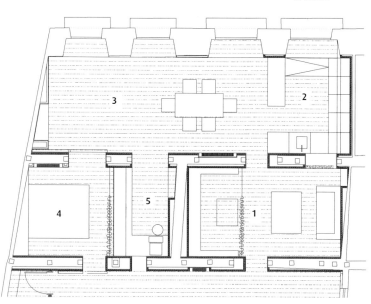

Loft in Plaza Mayor

Even though some elements of the original space were preserved, such as the dark wood platform, new materials transformed the character of the space by giving it a contemporary image. Designer furniture, like the chaise lounge by Le Corbusier upholstered in cowhide, complements the atmosphere.

The stainless steel table, which serves as a counter in the kitchen and as an informal dining room table, is a folding sheet attached to the wall that makes for continuity.

The openings in the walls create relationships between the various areas of the residence, such as the television room and the kitchen. The openings also take advantage of natural light to illuminate the spaces in the rear of the apartment.

Loft in Plaza Mayor

Alterations to an apartment in the Eixample

Bercedo + Mestre
Barcelona, Spain
Photography: Eugeni Pons

This project consists of alterations to a 1,026-square-foot apartment (plus a terrace of 130 square feet) in Barcelona's Eixample district. Like many apartments in the area, its characteristics are typical of those of the early 20th century. On the one hand, it features highly attractive elements: ceilings with timber beams and handmade vaults; considerable height between floor-ceiling structures; and large doors of wood and glass. On the other, it presents obvious defects: an obsolete distribution; clear disproportion between the depth (75 feet) and width (16 feet) of the dwelling; restricted entry of natural light at the ends; and ventilation of the rooms by means of badly lit inner patios. Consequently, the architects enhanced the presence of the more valuable elements and transformed defects into favorable qualities.

Alterations to an apartment in the Eixample

Potentiate advantages, reduce drawbacks

The first decision was to demolish all of the existing partitions, since the very depth of the apartment established a polarity between one end of the apartment and the other. In this way, differentiation between uses and different degrees of privacy was established not through real divisions, but through distance. The itinerary leading from the daytime to the nighttime zones, from private to shared areas, became the system by which the different environments of the dwelling are interrelated.

The wall is demolished

The natural light from the two ends of the apartment is transmitted by a system of transparencies: translucent glass panes that link spaces such as the study and the master bedroom, or the living room and the kitchen.

Around the recesses formed by the tiny inner patios, in the middle of the dwelling, stand the kitchen, a bathroom, and a toilet. In this way, the path through the apartment acquires an S shape that avoids a direct visual relationship between the daytime and nighttime zones. At the point of inflection, the ceiling has been lowered and the corridor has been narrowed to a minimal width, which acts as a counterpoint to the spaciousness of the remaining environments.

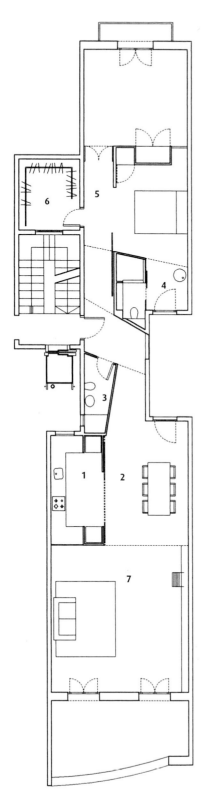

Sophisticated comfort

The shower and toilet stand where the apartment narrows due to the presence of the entrance and the small inner patio. Gresite provides a fresh, summer-like environment.

1. Kitchen

2. Dining room

3. Toilet

4. Bathroom

5. Bedroom

6. Wardrobe

7. Living room

Plan

Alterations to an apartment in the Eixample

Bishop's mansions apartment

Pablo Uribe
London, United Kingdom
Photography: Montse Garriga

This apartment's exceptional location, on the ground floor of a house in Fulham, London that dates back to 1900, provides an especially peaceful setting. The front yard, where the entrance is located, and the rear garden, which is shared with the rest of the neighborhood, provide all of the rooms with natural light, while the trees and shrubs grant a sense of tranquillity.

Renovation dramatically changed the interior configuration, achieving a feeling of spaciousness. As in the majority of Victorian houses, the space had been divided into rooms off of a long corridor. The architect eliminated all of the nonstructural walls and created a series of areas, from the front yard to the rear garden, where household activities can take place in a single setting.

The home's new configuration eliminated a second bedroom and used the space for the social area, and in the new bathroom, done in silver, the bathtub was sacrificed in favor of a large new shower.

To maintain an unobstructed traffic pattern, the master bedroom was connected with the rest of the apartment by a unique unit that serves two purposes: on one side, it is a wall and bed support, and on the other, it is an armoire that marks off the space used as a dressing room.

The architect drew his inspiration from the work of Adolf Loos, whose settings are known for their great warmth and visual richness, well suited to the London climate. Cherrywood was chosen for the cabinets and the wall paneling, and mahogany was used for the piece that separates the bed from the dressing room. In the kitchen, all of the appliances are hidden behind cherrywood doors, so the kitchen is fully integrated with the living and dining areas.

Bishop's mansions apartment

A collapsible table makes it possible to use the space next to the kitchen as a dining area or as another small living room integrated with the rest of the apartment.

Bishop's mansions apartment

Inviting atmosphere

Although the renovation completely breaks with the original Victorian style, it employs materials that connect with that architectural style. The unfinished brick, dark wood, and light colors help create a warm ambience.

Zen apartment

Various Architects
Milan, Italy
Photography: Interstampa

This apartment is a curious alternative within the range of possibilities available to architects and designers. With elements manufactured almost entirely in the West, an environment more characteristic of Japan than of Europe has been created, in terms both of spatial experience and of the kind of spatial experience and visual features.

The functional organization of this almost square apartment of some 970 square feet is at first sight simple. A wall divides it into two areas, separating the daytime from the nighttime zones. Access to the apartment is gained from the nighttime zone, beyond which lies its daytime equivalent. Left behind, to the right, are the master bedroom and the large bathroom and, to the left, the guest room (which can be used as a meditation room when there are no guests). In the daytime zone, and annexed to the guest room, we find the kitchen and a toilet, opposite which stands the living/dining room. This clear division into different spaces is

tempered by differences in level—
between the bathroom and the bedroom,
and between the dining and living areas—
and by the presence of movable panels or
shoji, which act as interior walls that in a
single gesture isolate certain spaces from
or communicate them with the rest of the
dwelling. The fact that these panels are
made of traditional parchment means
that, even when they are closed, they
allow a degree of visual communication,
thanks to their translucent quality.

The strict geometry, the colors—white, beige, black, red, blue—and the use of natural wood bring this apartment close to a distant and highly attractive culture.

The advantages of Japanese culture now also in the West

 # Japanese minimalism

Apartment in Sant Sadurní

Josep Juvé
Sant Sadurní, Spain
Photography: Eugeni Pons

In this apartment, architecture and decoration combine to form a complex, functional space. Both disciplines were reflected on simultaneously, so it is difficult to decide whether the different elements are the consequence of a structural, a functional, or a purely formal requirement. Essence and ornament cannot be disassociated, and are necessary to endow the dwelling with meaning.

The development of the project was based on fieldwork closely linked to improvisation. However, this does not mean that decisions were taken randomly; instead, that work progressed on the basis of previously chosen alternatives. Observation of what had been built nourished the new designs.

Besides the building itself and the furniture, special attention was paid to the finishes, particularly paint. All of the corners enjoy exclusive tones that highlight different details. The wall lamps, for example, stand out against the rest of

the vertical partitions. On the other hand, some of the walls feature inscriptions that play a twofold role: one semantic and the other visual. Similarly, the paint serves to falsify textures. Thus brick is dissolved in different pastel shades, while wood disappears behind gilt.

Poetics and imagination

Apartment in Sant Sadurní

FFUSCATE NO LE TUE
dro

Without complexes

The originality of this project lies in its sincerity. No devices were used to disguise installations, surfaces were treated to accentuate textures, and the cupboards reveal their contents, since only a few have doors. The perception of space, although rather chaotic, is frank and spontaneous.

Even the staircase changes in nature as it climbs. The first step is of wood, a kind of introduction, and this is followed by a pair of masonry steps that confer solidity on the structure. Farther up, the steps become malleable metal sheets that fold until the wooden mezzanine is reached. This element is a compendium of ideas that govern the project: a mixture of constructional details, materials, colors, textures, and finishes that form a heterogeneous ensemble, producing a multitude of sensations that enrich perception of the ambience.

Imaginative lighting

The illumination presents a number of different solutions. On the one hand, natural light enters through windows that vary in terms of transparency: the panes of treated glass differ in texture and opacity.
On the other hand, there are numerous lamps: some stand on the floor and give off a diffuse light; others are table lamps; and still others are "festival" lights purely for decoration, since the light they give off is merely referential.

Apartment on Flinders Lane

Staughton Architects
Melbourne, Australia
Photography: Shannon McGrath

This space is located in an old office building in the heart of Melbourne that was converted to an apartment complex. Since the building is elongated and on a corner, the apartments have windows facing the exterior, and vertical traffic is confined to the two ends. Although the exterior still looks the same as it did when the building was new—even the original windows were retained— the interior is surprising because of its contemporary design and warm atmosphere, reflecting the lifestyle in this district, which is undergoing an urban renewal process.

The project is defined by two principal elements. The first is a multifunctional, freestanding wood-framed unit that encloses the sleeping area, provides storage space, serves as an auxiliary dining room, includes bookshelves, and is a sculptural element in and of itself. This unit is self-supporting, touching neither the ceiling nor the lateral walls, and looks almost like a piece of furniture.

The second element is the set of patterns sandblasted into the original cement floor. These patterns, with their polished texture, are reminiscent of the diagrams used by the architects in their design plans and contrast with the previous floor covering.

The layout is very simple. The wood-and-polycarbonate unit dynamically divides the space. On the one hand, it separates the space into two clearly defined areas: bedroom and living room. On the other hand, it delimits the kitchen and guides traffic to the narrow entrance of the bedroom and the bathroom. The patterns on the floor simply suggest ways to approach the layout and, to accommodate the furnishings, the area was left completely open.

The industrial character of the space was maintained by retaining elements such as the original ventilation ducts, wrought iron, piping, and the original flooring.

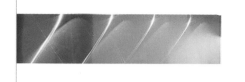

In addition to performing multiple functions, the polycarbonate-and-wood unit also acts as a lamp, behind which shadows are visible.

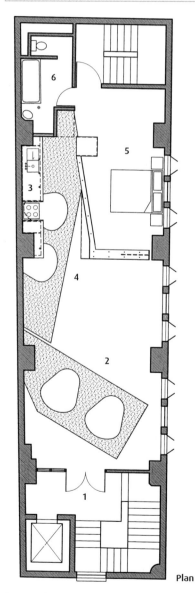

1. Entrance
2. Living room
3. Kitchen
4. Dining room
5. Bedroom
6. Bathroom

Plan

Apartment on Flinders Lane

The remodeling of an apartment

Salvador Villalba
Xàbia, Spain
Photography: Eugeni Pons

The truly brilliant aspect of this project by Salvador Villalba is its apparent simplicity. The obstacles he has had to overcome are disguised in the form of constructional details that enrich the perception of space without complicating it. The remodeling of this apartment in Xàbia (Alicante) includes the design of many of the pieces of furniture, the installation of a new system of artificial lighting, and the creation of a new building system that governs the layout.

Outstanding among the interventions is the treatment of the vertical partitions: while some have simply been painted or stuccoed, others have been clad in wood to endow the interior with a greater feeling of warmth. Still others, like the one in the living room, are of double thickness in order to accommodate installations and pieces of furniture encrusted in the wall. This mechanism has a unifying effect in that it formally melds architecture and interior design.

Sampaoli House

Claudio Caramel
Padua, Italy
Photography: Paolo Utimpergher

Created inside an old print shop, formerly used as a carpentry warehouse, this loft is located in a building in the center of Padua, in northern Italy. Though the space preserved its original character—the starting point for the intervention—the architect created an atmosphere that more closely matches the typology of a traditional residence. The private spaces are defined by independent bedrooms, but the area that dominates the interior is a large room that groups the functions of the living room, dining room, and kitchen.

The atmosphere of this space is a well-balanced mix of technology and creativity. The result is subtle elegance. The clarity of the forms was achieved through an ingenious strategy to hide certain elements and highlight others. The main entrance is through a garage that leads to the studio or to the residence, resolving the issue of parking while creating an unusual and informal entrance. The space containing the living room, dining room, and kitchen is a large atmosphere bathed in light, thanks to large windows and light-colored walls. As in the rest of the residence, traces of its former industrial use are visible, like the brick walls, exposed tubes, pillars painted white, and band of glass blocks in the upper part. The sleeping zone is delimited by walls and doors, as in a conventional residence, and includes two bedrooms and two bathrooms. These interiors stand out for their cleanliness and austere forms. Other highlights are the small-format tiles and the faucets and bathroom fixtures designed by Philippe Starck.

The materials give the space a homogeneous and natural appearance. For the living room floor, the architect used maple wood, while in the kitchen and bathrooms, there is smooth concrete painted with enamel. The final white finish reveals the original texture of the brick in some cases, and in others, it shows a peeled effect. Many of the lamps were designed by the owner. The furnishings, a combination of original historical pieces and recycled elements, constitute the final touch of this space with fine details.

1. Access/garage
2. Kitchen
3. Dining room
4. Bathroom
5. Bedroom

Plan

Details

The exact measurements of the design details of the interior architecture and the use of a certain type of furniture inside the space give this project a somewhat informal and casual appearance, though with truly contemporary taste.

This interior's casual and informal image was achieved through the combination of austere furnishings, pieces designed by the owner of the residence, and some industrial elements, like the metallic shelves for books and the kitchen cabinets.

Sampaoli House

Even though the private zones—the bedrooms and the bathrooms—are not part of the general space, they have a similar character. The humid zone of the bathroom is defined by mosaic that covers part of the walls, as if in a superimposed drawing.

Claudio Caramel

Apartment in white

Arthur Collin
London, United Kingdom
Photographs: Richard Glover

White interior spaces are a commonplace, a custom, a convenience. White is the chromatic base par excellence. Aware of this, Arthur Collin has designed an apartment in which white not only predominates, but also is the absolute protagonist. Based on the fact that there is no single white, the project emphasizes the subtle differences between three different whites. Unlike the cold effect of minimalist white, the variations between these tones endow the dwelling with warmth.

The apartment is the result of the remodeling of an attic in a Georgian building. The house was totally altered in the 1970s, so it became possible to insert an entirely contemporary interior without coming across original elements of a certain historical value.

Space flexibility

The living room cupboards extend until they reach the kitchen, where they accommodate the appliances. This piece of furniture unites the two spaces, although the composition of the doors endows each zone with its own character. The handles are slots, so that the surface, though smooth and monolithic, is seen to be geometrical and textured.

The bookcase on the stairs is an ingenious mechanism consisting of 13 old boxes painted in three tones of white. Thanks to this mechanism, there was no need to build banisters.

With this project, Arthur Collin shows that such a common, basic color as white is capable of endowing a space with character. This London architect has carried the use of white to the limit, and the result is a comfortable, warm, entirely contemporary home.

Apartment in white

The kitchen consists of an L-shaped unit that includes the sink and the stainless steel hood. The folding table is made of recycled plastic, a mixture of detergent bottles that may be appreciated in the different tones of the surface.

Energy-efficient apartment

Lichtblau & Wagner
Vienna, Austria
Photography: Andreas Wagner, Margherita Spiluttinl

The reconversion of this attic in Vienna is characterized by the application of energy-saving ideas hitherto adapted only to other architectural domains. While in residential architecture the main concerns were functional or aesthetic aspects, Lichtblau & Wagner has introduced concepts of energy efficiency and economy into this field. In order to achieve energy saving, these young Austrian architects have ruled out all superficial luxuries, marble bathrooms, pointless terraces, and grandiose entrances to concentrate on a flexible project that economizes on energy, budget, and space.

Four basic units, 540 square feet each, were organized in pairs and with an additional space that may be added to one apartment or the other. This alteration is easy to achieve, thanks to the simple relocation of partitions.

The project offers flexibility in the use of space. The available surface area is maximal, since circulation zones have been eliminated. The different areas may be used for different activities during the day and throughout the year. The maximum exponent of this idea is the space beneath sliding windows, since depending on the weather, it may be used as a terrace, a gallery, or a greenhouse. Curtains separate this space thermally from the rest of the dwelling, and create a sensation of warmth and comfort.

Energy efficient apartment

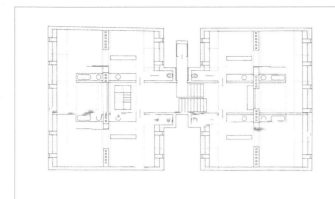

The solar panels provide eight apartments with hot water, and the centralized heating system produces a saving in terms of both energy and space. Good thermal insulation and passive solar energy contribute to reduced heating and cooling costs.

From the constructional point of view, the absence of interior walls contributes to reducing costs. Moreover, the electrical installations are in the floor, thus eliminating the need for sockets in the vertical partitions. The kitchen and bathroom units are collapsible, and are connected to the drains through holes in the flooring. In this way, their positions may be interchanged, or they may simply be removed when not needed.

Compact living

Lichtblau & Wagner's bathrooms are linked to the living areas. They are not conceived as hermetic units, they are lit by natural light, and from them it is possible to view the daytime areas.

L House

Sauerbruch & Hutton
London, United Kingdom; Photography: Michael Claus,
Katsuhida Kida, Hélène Binet, Charlie Stebbings

Sauerbruch & Hutton was required to remodel this old, conventional, Victorian semidetached house in London. The building, the four floors of which total a surface area of around 1,836 square feet, was redesigned to contain offices on the first two floors and a dwelling on the remaining two floors above. The clients in this case were the architects themselves. The reconversion work revealed how the concept of space—or of mentality, which amounts to the same thing—had evolved from Victorian times to the early 1990s, when the project was executed. During the latter half of the 19th century, building interiors were usually divided into many closed, centripetal spaces. In contrast, at the end of the 20th century the trend was to obtain practical, open, diaphanous space in which there is often an interplay—visual and physical— between the different zones of the project and between the project and its surroundings. With minimal gestuality,

Sauerbruch & Hutton has achieved excellent results. After a vertical itinerary in which sensations increase in intensity as we climb, the climax is reached precisely on the top floor: all partitions having been eliminated, the floor is completely open plan, and the living room, dining room, and kitchen constitute a single space. All this beneath a totally glazed gable roof that replaces the original structure.

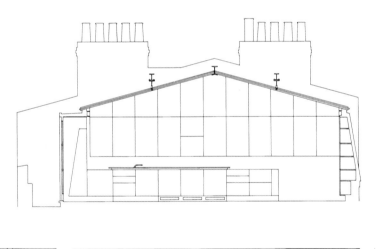

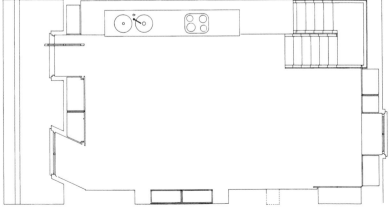

The decision to open the building through the roof—a triumph in this latitude, where natural light is scarce—places the project in contact with a unique, ever-changing, and enormously attractive landscape: the London sky. The celestial vault is thus converted into a kind of extension of the dwelling, a private "garden." During the day, natural light floods the interior, either directly or filtered through curtains. Later on, at dusk, a column of artificial light rises up from this top floor to be lost, creating a theatrical effect in the darkness of the night.

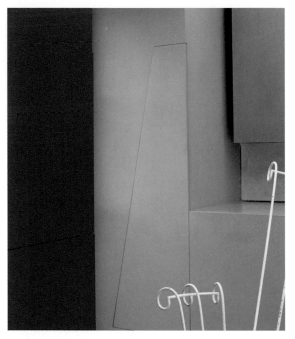

 # The celestial garden

The use of color and textures is a further characteristic of this project. Bright colors, warm wood surfaces, and fine cladding endow this apartment with a high degree of comfort: a perfect example of Sauerbruch & Hutton's intelligence and spirit of sensuality when it comes to reinterpreting—imposing the architects' own character on—an existing space.

The project is partially characterized by the search for balance between functionalism, the need for privacy, and free flow from one space to the next. In this context, the strategic placing of cupboards plays a fundamental role, since in this way storage space is restricted to specific areas, freeing the rest of the floor. On the one hand, we find cupboards all along the perimeter, taking advantage of the outer wall recesses; on the other, they appear as separating elements between rooms, rather like partitions.

Attic in São Paulo

Arthur de Mattos Casas
São Paulo, Brazil
Photography: Tuca Reinés

The work of Arthur de Mattos Casas encompasses many disciplines, so it is hard to gauge the extent of the influence of his creative activity. A hunter of ideas, just like a Renaissance man—artist, architect, craftsman, and philosopher—this versatile Brazilian strives to achieve a solid, coherent relationship between space and the objects that occupy it. And what better way to achieve this than by designing both elements? The place and the utensils serve the needs of this space, both functionally and visually.

The interior design process in this and other projects by de Mattos Casas is marked by a counterpoint between the purity of rationalism and the sumptuousness of decoration. Rationalism defends formal essence against ornament. This apartment is evidence of the fact that both trends may exist harmoniously side by side.

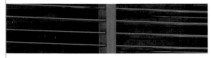

Architecture, design, and craft work

The merit of a holistic approach to architecture, design, and craft work lies in having unified these elements into a single concept, in having designed objects that allow a certain poetic license in details.

Arthur de Mattos Casas

This apartment in São Paulo occupies the top two floors of a building and enjoys magnificent views over the city. The dining room and living room are closed to the exterior via a mesh of wooden slats, which protect the interior from direct sunlight and provide greater privacy. The lighting is one of the most carefully conceived elements of the project. Warm, uniform lighting was designed, together with points of light that bring certain places to the fore, either for functional reasons or to feature an object or work of art.

Attic in São Paulo

Inlaid work and the use of different types of wood, for both structural and ornamental elements, return here. The stairs joining the two levels are an example of innovation in the use of wood. The staircase consists of steps in the form of drawers, whose structural raison d'être lies in the way each one rests on the one below. In this way an almost sculptural object of extreme elegance is obtained.

Arthur de Mattos Casas

 # Poetic details

The kitchen and bathrooms are the product of simple, forceful design. The effort to minimize complicated forms contributes to the fact that the more functional parts of the apartment are extremely practical, while retaining their identity and harmonizing with the overall style.

Attic in São Paulo

Space for two

Guillermo Arias
Cartagena de Indias, Colombia
Photography: Carlos Tobón

This small, recreational apartment designed for a couple occupies what were once two living rooms in an old residence in a 1930s building in Cartagena de Indias. The building is located in Santo Domingo Plaza, one of the most emblematic spaces in the city. Despite the apartment's splendid views of the plaza and the church, the interior was run-down and was divided by a confusing and disorganized series of exposed beams.

The first step was to reproduce the atmosphere that most likely existed in the original space, but with a contemporary feel. A series of large moldings define the general space, which is now continual and free of dividing walls. Various architectural elements make up the different areas and disguise the central column that forms part of the structure. Just after the entrance is a space that contains the kitchen, dining room, and living room. This area ends with a window overlooking the plaza. The kitchen is designed as an isolated table that contains all of the appliances and also functions as the dining room table. A low wall, with an incorporated bookshelf, connects this space to the bedroom. A sliding door made with strips of wood and interfacing also makes it possible to divide the areas. The bathroom is found at the back of the bedroom. The headboard of the bed separates the bathroom from the bedroom and also functions as a closet. A double sink defines the bathroom's social and private areas. The toilets feature the same symmetry as the sinks, and there is a central shower. Almost all of the details of the furnishings are incorporated into the interior architecture. The architect, Guillermo Arias, designed most of the furnishings himself, including the shelves, the marble countertop in the bathroom, the kitchen cabinets, and all of the lamps. Arias is well known for his attention to detail—gestures that enrich this small space and give it formal unity.

Volumetric play

The transformation of this apartment into a single atmosphere with diverse functions was resolved by creating different spaces that relate to one another and define the functions of the residence. The moldings, low walls, horizontal planes, and niches were carefully studied to create aesthetic and functional harmony.

1. Entry
2. Kitchen
3. Bathroom
4. Dining room
5. Bedroom

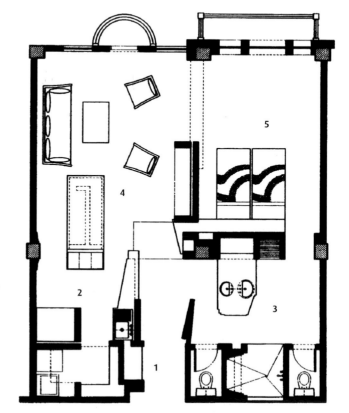

Plan

The false depth of the walls creates a dialogue with the original spacious character of the apartment. Niches used as shelves are incorporated into the architecture itself.

The lamps, designed by the architect, feature bronze, antique crystal, and alabaster, alluding to the space's original classic style.

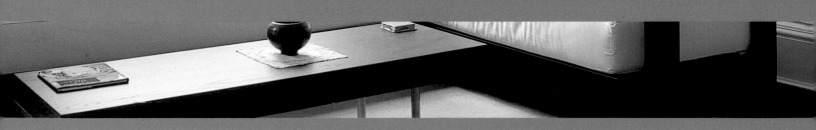

Horizontal unit

Stephen Quinn & Elise Ovanessoff
London, United Kingdom
Photography: Jordi Miralles

This apartment is located in a typical four-story Georgian house in the neighborhood of Marylebone in central London. This project entailed remodeling the first floor, which was originally a reception area. Previous renovations were of poor quality, so the architects decided to re-create the original space and adapt it to a new, more efficient use.

The apartment consisted of two different atmospheres connected with some steps. The architects first restored the large room at the front to its former size and moved the kitchen to a more convenient location. The bedroom is located in the back and leads to a walk-in closet with a sliding door painted with green-and-blue stripes. The bathroom was carefully designed to accommodate all of the necessities. The bed is made of wood and has four drawers below that complement the closet as additional storage space. As a result, the bedroom is uncluttered and gives the sensation of open space.

The furnishings in the large front room have dark tones. A desk of lacquered wood and four black chairs define the dining room, and the living room includes a sofa, in the form of an L with white cushions, and a low table. The walls are white and all of the decorative elements are limited to objects, sculptures, and statuettes placed on top of tables. Certain elements, such as the chimney and the large windows, refer to the spirit of the old house. A key feature of this project is the use of space and light, which, combined with the high ceilings, transform this small apartment into a modern and practical home. The sparse use of color mixes with the solid, dark floors to create the impression of contrast.

The finished interior of this small loft still has traces of the original Georgian house built 200 years ago. Nevertheless, the architects have managed to create a completely modern apartment with comfortable and practical surroundings.

Two colors

The concept of chiaroscuro unifies the loft by giving the floors impact and by lightening the upper part of the atmosphere. Dark tones are used for the floors, the tables, the chairs, and everything else that makes up the lower part of the space. White, the contrasting color, is used for all of the walls, cushions, and textures of the upper part.

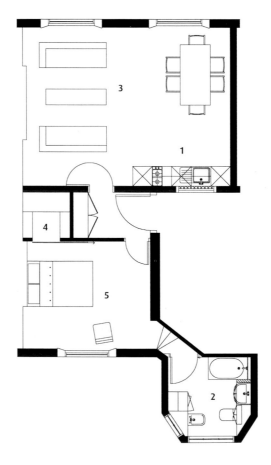

1. Kitchen
2. Bathroom
3. Dining room
4. Closet
5. Bedroom

Plan

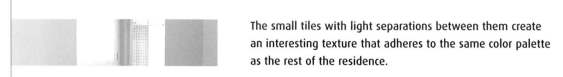

The small tiles with light separations between them create an interesting texture that adheres to the same color palette as the rest of the residence.

Horizontal unit

Spatial relations

McDonnell Associates Ltd
London, United Kingdom
Photography: Carlos Domínguez

This apartment, located in the center of London, was originally a structure without a ceiling that the owner wanted to remodel into a place where he could escape from the hustle and bustle of the city. The best features of the space, natural light and splendid views from the windows, are emphasized in this renovation.

The project's main challenge was to give the apartment mobility, so that the lighting or the structure of the atmospheres could be altered with little effort. To achieve this goal, the architect used light elements that are easily maneuvered. The solutions include curtains that diffuse the light; a pivoting, horizontal door that separates the kitchen from the dining room—inspired by garage doors; and a pivoting, vertical door that separates the living room from the glass staircase. The staircase and the living room are linked by a revolving wooden door with an axis in the center that turns 360 degrees, making

McDonnell Associates Ltd.

it a decorative object that enriches the space. The stainless steel kitchen provides an industrial feel, and can become part of the living/dining room, thanks to a panel that can be raised and lowered. The mixture of different materials, according to the characteristics of each space, enriches the overall atmosphere. The second floor is reached by way of glass stairs that allow the light to filter through. On the top floor, we find the bedroom, the bathroom, and a small living area that is connected to the lower floor with a metallic staircase. In contrast to the glass and metal, the wood flooring unifies the entire space. For the bathrooms, the architect used slate on the upper floor and marble on the entrance level. Wood covers the doors and some walls, giving the atmosphere warmth. Various mirrors generate a sensation of open space. In both bathrooms, there are built-in sinks of matted glass with classic fixtures. Glass closets lighten the space. In this London apartment, the diverse materials and the relationship between the different areas, which can be modified according to the layout, generate a functional home with spatial richness.

Pivoting doors

The wooden door that links the main living room with the staircase leading to the top-floor living and sleeping areas has a pivot in the center of its frame, producing a double entrance. The stainless steel door that divides the kitchen from the dining room can be adjusted to restrict or increase the opening between these two spaces.

Stainless steel materials and the color white were chosen to reflect the light and enhance the sense of open space.

The bathrooms include materials such as marble, slate, glass, and mirrors that, through their placement, create optical effects that amplify the small space.

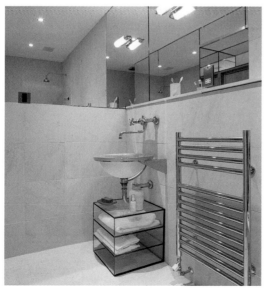

Apartment with a terrace in Manhattan

Shelton, Mindel & Associates
New York, United States
Photography: Michael Moran

The first step in this 2,160 square foot apartment project was to detect those problems that required specific solutions. Thus the following priorities were established: to integrate project and city; to take maximum advantage of the four facades and the roof; and to house a collection of pieces of furniture and objets d'art by 20th-century artists and architects.

On the lower level of the apartment, public and private spaces are very clearly differentiated. The zone most suitable for public relations is the south facade, organized around an element in the form of a water tank. A large living room, with a fireplace, and a dining room, with an annexed zone in which to sit, are located on either side of the central artifact, a circular space and glass box with a double spiral stainless steel staircase.

The public and the private, independent

On the west facade, an irregular volume contains the elevator and a storeroom. Furthermore, an L-shaped services strip separates this more public space from the private areas. Part of the L, which contains the vertical communications nucleus, the entrance to the apartment, a toilet, and the kitchen—which opens into the dining room—occupies the east facade. The other part, with a bathroom and dressing room for the two single bedrooms and another for the double bedroom, creates an intermediate zone between the bedrooms—with excellent views north—and the rest of the apartment.

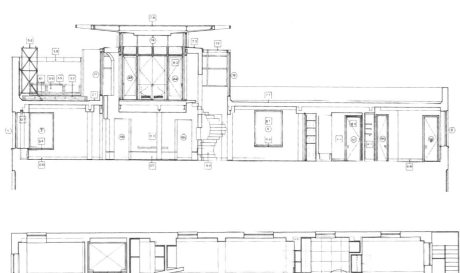

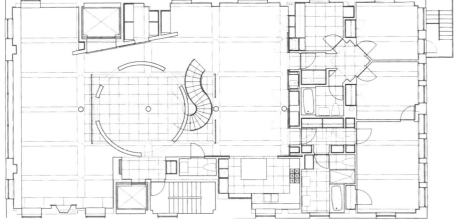

Shelton, Mindel & Associates

In the apartment, the mobile panels acquire a certain importance, since the fact that they may be opened or closed modifies the perception of space. Aluminum, stainless steel, structural white glass, and oak and cherry wood on the floors are some of the materials used for this apartment. Jean Prouvé, Richard Serra, Arnold Hoffman, Robert Jacobsen, Alvar Aalto, Charles Eames, Caldés, Wagner, and Robert Ryman are some of the artists, sculptors, ceramists, and architects whose works are exhibited inside.

In a single gesture, the spiral staircase resolves access to the roof. The enclosed volume makes it possible to link the lower floor—specifically its more public zone—with the roof and the sky, creating a living room on the level above. This volume may also be used as an exhibition space.

Apartment with a terrace in Manhattan

A space for one of their own

Shelton, Mindel & Associates has invested all of its talents in this apartment for one member of the team, Lee Mindel, as well as all of its capacity to detect problems to be faced.

Shelton, Mindel & Associates

Playful and intimate

Gary Chang/EDGE (HK) LTD
Hong Kong, China
Photography: Almond Chu

This apartment, located in Hong Kong, was designed by architect Gary Chang as his personal residence. Located in a popular neighborhood, this old flat was previously the home of a large family. The goal of the project was to create a space that, despite its reduced proportions, contains all of the necessary residential functions, yet has flexibility for rest and leisure.

In order to make the most of the principal window located in the back part of the residence, the architect grouped the bathroom, kitchen, and laundry room in the front. As a result, the main space could enjoy the window, the best source of natural light. As an empty space, it could also accommodate diverse uses as the bedroom, living room, study, and video room. To achieve flexibility in such a small area, Chang combined light divisions, carefully planned lighting, and mobile furnishings. All of his possessions for work and leisure, such as books, videos, and disks, as well as the

home's accessories, are stored in a system of metallic shelves that are discreetly hidden behind white curtains. The result is that the central space can accommodate all of the daytime and nighttime activities with the simple movement of one or several curtains. The architect used transparent and white translucent materials. By combining them with mood lighting, he gave the apartment a quality of lightness in which the materials seem to vanish. To tone down the rigidity of the floor and make it more ethereal, Chang and his collaborators used fluorescent tubes on one side and a more brilliant light that articulates the structural parts on the other. The only heavy object, at least in appearance, is the solid cherrywood tower that contains the projector, refrigerator, kitchen, bathroom, and washing machine. The principal opening of the window offers different possibilities since a screen for television, video, and Internet can extend over it. Each detail was carefully thought out and designed with the objective of making the most of every corner of this 323-square-foot space. In this single atmosphere, the architect managed to group residential necessities in a simple and elegant way. The lights and the convertible elements alter the apartment for different circumstances, adding a playful yet relaxed spirit.

Projection

The small proportions of this space seem to vanish, thanks to the layout, which faces the back window. At times, the space has the atmosphere of a small cinema. The apartment turns into a platform from which to contemplate the urban landscape or to watch a film.

The top shelves, hidden behind the curtains, are suspended from the wall. The lower shelves are supported by a fine metallic structure that complements the lightness of the space.

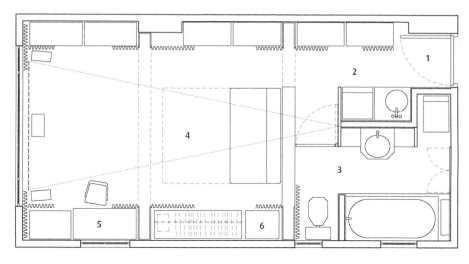

1. Entry
2. Kitchen
3. Bathroom
4. Living room/
   bedroom
5. Studio
6. Cabinet

Plan

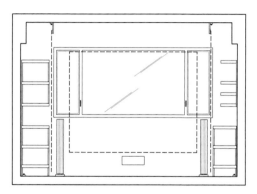

Transversal section of the living room

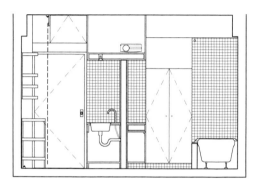

Transversal section of the bathroom and kitchen

Playful and intimate

Despite the small space, the architect achieved great formal expressiveness in the bathroom area. This space combines design elements, like fixtures by Philippe Starck, with economical solutions such as lighting from two fluorescent tubes.

The placement of each piece of furniture breaks traditional schemes and produces diverse spatial relationships in the same atmosphere.